One hundred and one ideas for creative prayers

for group use

Judith Merrell

Illustrations by Anna Carpenter

Scripture Union

Special Occasions

Scripture Union, 207–209 Queensway, Bletchley, MK2 2EB, England.

Text © Judith Merrell 1995
Illustrations © Anna Carpenter 1995

First published 1995, reprinted 1998, 2001

ISBN 0 86201 9540

British Library
Cataloguing-in-Publication Data.
A catalogue record for this book is available from the British Library.

Designed by Tony Cantale Graphics

Printed and bound in Great Britain by Cox and Wyman Ltd, Reading.

Contents

Introduction

SO WHAT'S IT ALL ABOUT?

Many children are taught to recite prayers 'parrot fashion' from a very early age. They might learn a mealtime grace or The Lord's Prayer, in exactly the same way that they learn a nursery rhyme, but do they ever learn who they are talking to and do they understand the meaning of the words they repeat?

You've probably heard young children pray 'Our Father who art in heaven, Harold be thy name...' It's a common mistake to make since children will often insert familiar words with a similar sound in place of words that have no meaning for them. A small four year old was once heard to pray, with great sincerity, 'Our Father who's Martin Evans...' Well, there were three children called Martin in her kindergarten class so it was an understandable mistake! It is vitally important that we take the time to explain the whole concept of prayer to children young and old, so that they grow up confident that they can talk to God easily and naturally about whatever is on their hearts.

Have you ever tried to explain prayer, what it is and how you do it? It's no easy task! Take a couple of minutes to think about it now. What words and expressions would you use?

Many years ago I remember hearing prayer described as 'like a telephone conversation with God'. Yet prayer is something far better than that. God is never out or too busy to answer our call. We don't need to queue for the phone. We don't need to pay peak rates for daytime conversations and we don't need to worry about how we're going to pay the bill at the end of the quarter! Cliff Richard dispenses with all these problems and describes prayer in the following helpful words: 'Prayer is like instant telephone calls to God. You don't even need a telephone! All you've got to do is think in your head what you want to say to him and he hears it.' (*The Piccolo Book of Prayers.*)

Once we have explained what prayer is, youngsters then want to know why we pray. We need to explain that God wants us to be in constant touch with him and, just as we chat to our friends, so God wants us to talk to him. God chooses to work through people's prayers and in this way he gives us the opportunity to play a part in the good things he does. We also pray because the Bible specifically tells us to. See Ephesians 6:18-19; Philippians 4:6; Colossians 4:2; 1 Thessalonians 5:16-18; 1 Timothy 2:1,2; James 5:13,14.

When I was a child, prayer time at my junior school was always introduced by the words, 'Hands together and eyes closed.' It was all part of an accepted ritual. We didn't listen to the words that followed. I'm not sure that we even understood them, we just waited for the word 'Amen' which was the cue to open our eyes. I often wonder how many children have grown up with the assumption that 'Amen' means 'You can open your eyes now'! While familiar routines offer the comfort of a security blanket, they can also leave people thinking that there is only one correct way to pray. Years of listening to other people pray on their behalf can leave youngsters with the impression that only ministers and Sunday group leaders can talk to God. Equally, if all our prayers begin with 'Most Almighty Father God' and end with 'Amen' youngsters may well assume that this is the secret formula that makes a prayer work! Misunderstandings gleaned at an early age can take a long while to shake off.

It is important that leaders don't just pray on behalf of children or adults, but encourage them to participate as well. It is all too easy to switch off when someone else is praying! Moreover, if leaders always pray at great length and pepper all their prayers with long and learned words, those listening may well be left feeling 'I could never do that!' It is therefore essential that we find ways of encouraging others to pray both on their own and in groups.

The following 101 creative prayer ideas have been divided into four sections. The first section 'But I don't know what to pray' includes ideas for how you might structure and stimulate sessions for a time of group prayer. The second section 'Prayers to join in' includes a number of response prayers where a leader and the group or congregation pray alternately. The third section 'Prayers to shout out loud' includes a handful of prayer shouts and chants. The last and largest section 'Prayers to write, draw, and make' covers prayer collages, praise posters and many other creative prayer suggestions that can be used either with groups of youngsters or in situations where all ages meet to pray together.

If you are looking for a prayer for a particular event or festival, there is a 'Special Occasions' index at the front of the book. You will also find a complete list of all the 101 prayer ideas in the section entitled 'Contents'.

With thanks to the writers of *Learning Together with 7 to 11s* and *SALT: 8 to 10+* who have inspired several of the ideas in this book and to all those who have allowed their work to be used. Every effort has been made to attribute items correctly, but I apologise to any author whose work has not been credited. Please inform the publisher and this will be rectified in any future editions of *101 creative prayer ideas for groups*.

Bible verses quoted are taken from The Good News Bible.

Section One

BUT I DON'T KNOW WHAT TO PRAY...

Many groups feel that they would like
to have a time of open prayer as part of their weekly meeting,
but for many children and some adults this can be a daunting
prospect. They'd rather not join in because they don't know
what to pray about. A short time of discussion can provide a
natural lead-in to prayers.

Sometimes people find it helpful to have
some kind of structure on which they can base
their discussion and the prayers that follow. You might
like to try out some of the following ideas.

1. Thank you, sorry, please (teaspoon prayers)

Perhaps the most simple way of structuring a prayer is to use the three words thank you, sorry and please. Have a short time of chat and discussion focusing on what the group might want to say to God using these three words. Finally have a short time of open prayer or ask a leader to weave together all the topics mentioned, in a closing prayer. TSP, the first letters of Thank you, Sorry, Please, remind us of the recipe book abbreviation for teaspoon. It can be helpful to give younger children a plastic teaspoon to take home to remind them of these three basic categories for prayer.

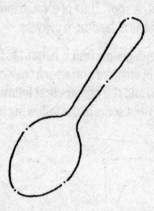

2. Three envelopes

Some groups start out by being rather shy about praying out loud. In this case why not pin up three envelopes labelled 'Thank you', 'Sorry' and 'Please' and let group members write their prayers on slips of paper and put them in the appropriate envelope. Don't forget to check the envelopes from time to time to let everyone share in the joy of the thank you prayers and to find out how the please prayers have been answered.

3. Prayer bookmarks

Youngsters often grow up with all kinds of misunderstandings about prayer. Some children believe that only important folk like Archbishops and Sunday Group leaders can pray. Others think that you can only pray about big, important issues. Some children think that it is wrong to pray in the middle of the night because God might be asleep and one or two believe that God will only hear you if you pray in church. Why not make prayer bookmarks (see illustration) to help your group remember that God does not restrict where, when and how we can pray.

Encourage children to copy out the following short prayer on side one of the bookmark:

> Lord God,
> Thank you that wherever I am,
> Whatever the time,
> I can pray about anything at all,
> Big or small!
> Amen

On side two get the children to write:

> ANYONE can PRAY
> about ANYTHING,
> ANY TIME, ANYWHERE.

Let children decorate their bookmarks with drawings or sticky shapes. Then, punch a hole at the bottom and attach a tassel.

4. Prayer hand

Some people find it helpful to pray around the fingers of their hand. The index finger, which people generally use to point the way, reminds us to pray for the people who point the way for us in our lives, eg teachers and church leaders. The middle finger, which is taller than the others, reminds us to pray for those who rule over us. The third finger, on which many adults wear a wedding ring, reminds us to pray for those whom we love. The little finger, which is the weakest, reminds us to pray for those who are weak, elderly or ill. It can also remind us to pray for 'little old me'! Finally the thumb, which is set apart from the fingers, reminds us to pray for those abroad, missionaries or people living in difficult situations.

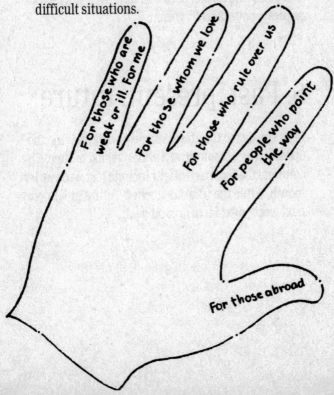

5. Yesterday, today, tomorrow

Divide a piece of paper into three columns and ask the group to tell you about anything that happened yesterday which they would like to give thanks for. Do the same for today and then move on to tomorrow, asking whether there is anything happening tomorrow that the group would like to request special prayers for. Make brief notes in each column and then move on to a time of open prayer. As each thing is prayed for tick it off so that everyone can see which items remain. It is often a good idea to ask a leader to close in prayer so that any items not yet mentioned can be included at this point and no one need feel that their prayer requests have been forgotten.

6. Past, present, future

Very similar to the above suggestion, but giving the opportunity of looking at a wider period of time. The column labelled 'past' might include last week or last month, while the column labelled 'future' might cover next week, next term or next year.

7. Four faces

The four faces illustrated below can work as a very effective prayer reminder. Draw each face on a separate piece of paper. Then show the faces to your group, one at a time, to prompt their suggestions for prayer. The first picture reminds us to begin by looking up to God and offering him our praise and worship. In the second picture the eyes are looking down. This reminds us to look at ourselves and pray about our own lives, thanking God for all the good things that have happened and saying sorry for all our wrongdoing. In the third picture the eyes are looking to one side. This reminds us to look around at others and to pray for our friends and for those who are ill or absent. Finally, in the fourth picture, the eyes are looking forward to the future. This reminds us to pray about some of the things that will be happening tomorrow, next week or next month.

8. Circle prayer

Ask your group to stand in a circle and hold hands. Then, in a few moments of silence, ask everyone to pray, first for the person on their left and then for the person on their right. Alternatively, if your group is quite confident about praying out loud, you might like to go round the group and ask each person to pray a short prayer for the person on their left, thanking God for him and asking that God would bless him. Why not finish by singing *Bind us together, Lord.* (Bob Gillman © Thankyou music)

9. Prayer and music mix

Some people find it hard to concentrate when prayers run on for a long time. Why not intersperse prayers and music?

Invite the group to sing a chorus or hymn with three or four verses and ask two or three people to contribute one short prayer in between each verse. Give each person a specific topic for their prayer (eg friends and family, the church and its organisations, the country and its leaders, international needs) and, if necessary, encourage them to write down their prayer beforehand. Some choruses are particularly well-suited to this treatment, eg *Father, I place into your hands the things that I can't do* (J. Hewer © Thankyou Music), *Father, we adore you* (Terrye Coelhoe © Maranatha Music). Both songs can be found in *Junior Praise* published by Marshall Pickering.

10. Prayer pauses

Many people find it helpful when prayers that are led from the front include short pauses for private prayer.

Father God, we thank you for our church/group and we ask that you will help us to grow closer to each other and closer to you.
Let's think of the people sitting on either side of us and ask that God will be especially close to them. (PAUSE)

We also remember those people who are not with us today, perhaps through illness or because they are on holiday.
Let's remember them in our own prayers now. (PAUSE)

Father God, we thank you for the town where we live and we ask that you will help us to spread your love to our friends and neighbours.
Let's think of one or two particular friends and ask that God will help us tell them the Good News. (PAUSE)

Father God, we thank you for the time we have spent together and we ask that you will be with us throughout the rest of the day.
Let's all think of the things that we are going to do later today and bring them before God now. (PAUSE)

Lord, thank you that you listen to all our prayers spoken and unspoken. Amen.

11. Three circles

Draw three circles, one inside the other, on a large sheet of paper. Label the inside circle 'our neighbourhood' and ask your group to suggest local issues that should be prayed about. Make one or two notes in this circle to remind everyone of the topics for prayer. Then label the second circle 'our country' and this time ask your group to suggest national topics for prayer and note down their ideas. Finally label the third circle 'other countries' and talk about and make notes on international topics for prayer. Finish with a short time of open prayer. Alternatively, ask a leader to weave together all the topics mentioned into a concluding prayer.

(Eileen Turner)

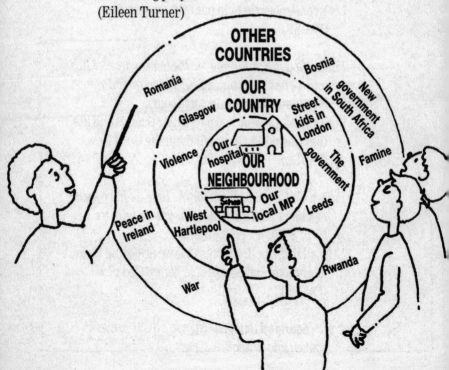

12. The church

Draw a simple outline of your church building and inside, on the left hand side, write the days of the week. Then, working through the seven days of the week, ask your group to name the different organisations that use your church buildings each day, eg Girls'/Boys' Brigade, mother and toddler group, prayer group, youth club, Sunday club. Pray for each group in turn asking that God will bless them in all their activities and that each group will come to know him better. If your group are used to praying aloud, you might like to ask different people to say a short prayer for each of the groups that meets on your church premises.

Sunday	**Church, Sunday Club, 18+ Group**
Monday	**Mother and Toddler Group**
Tuesday	**Girls' Brigade**
Wednesday	**Prayer Group, Badminton Club**
Thursday	**Boys' Brigade**
Friday	**Trailblazers**
Saturday	**Youth Club**

13. Prayer diaries

A prayer diary can often be used to encourage youngsters to pray regularly. Give each member of your group a piece of paper which they must divide into four columns. Leave the first column blank and put the headings, 'Thank you', 'Sorry' and 'Please' at the top of the remaining columns.

Write the seven days of the week in the first column and rule a line under each day. See illustration. Encourage your group to take the diaries home and spend a few minutes each evening writing a short thank you, sorry and please prayer about the events of the day.

	Thankyou	Sorry	Please
Sunday	for this wonderful weather	that I was in a bad mood this morning	look after my grandma in hospital
Monday			
Tuesday			
Wednesday			
Thursday			
Friday			
Saturday			

14. News time

Have a short time of sharing in which each group member briefly relates what they have been doing during the past week and what they expect to be doing during the coming week.

Make sure that no one feels that their news is too insignificant. God is interested in every aspect of our lives, not just the things that we consider to be important. Let this news time lead into a time of prayer, thanking God for the good things that have happened, asking God to bless those events which are still to come and asking him to help in those situations that are a cause for concern. You may like to have a short time of open prayer in which several people pray for one or two of the items mentioned.

Alternatively, you might prefer to have a time of silence in which each person quietly goes round the group, praying for the group members in turn as they remember what they said.

15. News headlines

Tape the news headlines from the radio just before you meet with your group. Listen to the recording together and then pray for those items mentioned on the news. Point out that amidst all the bad news in the world Christians have an important message of good news to tell others.

16. Prayer clusters

Christian adults often pray in small groups, but for youngsters this can be a daunting prospect. To help children feel at home with this practice, it is a good idea to give them a few guidelines to begin with.

Divide the children into groups of four or five and ask them to all think about one really good thing that happened to them last week. When they have had a few moments to think, ask them to tell the rest of the group what it was. Next ask the children to think ahead to the coming week and ask them to think if there is a particular event that they are concerned or excited about and to share this with the rest of the group. Then suggest that each child in the group says a short prayer for the child on their right. It might go something like this.

'Dear Lord, thank you that Jenny had a really good time with her friends at the swimming pool last week. Please help her not to feel nervous about going to the dentist on Tuesday. Amen.'

17. Walkabout

Many people find it hard to concentrate when they are sitting still. In fact some people can concentrate more easily when they are on their feet and moving around. Why not try out the following idea which enables people to move around as they pray.

Have ready a number of sheets of A4 paper and a marker pen. Ask group members to share anything for which they want to say 'Thank you', 'Sorry' or 'Please' to God. Write each suggestion in large lettering on a sheet of A4 paper. You might like to add to these sheets any prayer requests from mission partners attached to your church and also prayer pointers about situations in the news. These could be accompanied by photos and news clippings and should be prepared beforehand. Display these prayer requests around your room, spaced as far apart as possible. Invite the group to walk around, stopping from time to time to read the sheets and to pray silently for each item. You might like to play some very quiet music in the background.

18. Scrapbook

Why not keep a large prayer scrapbook for your group?
Begin with a short time of news and chat in which
group members share some of the joys and worries of
the previous week and any concerns that they have for
the following week. Then, ask a leader to weave all
these ideas into a prayer thanking God for all the good
things that have happened and asking for his help in
areas of concern. Write each prayer in marker pen on a
blank page in the scrapbook, so that the whole group
can read the prayer aloud together. Don't forget to date
each prayer as it is written. From time to time look
back over earlier pages and think about how God has
answered the prayer requests.
(Barbara and Andy Riordan)

Section Two

PRAYERS TO JOIN IN

All too often at church and in Sunday groups
someone at the front says the prayers on behalf of everyone else.
With the best will in the world I try hard to concentrate, but if the
prayers are too long or too wordy my attention starts to wander
and I come to just in time to join in with the final 'Amen'! If I, as
an adult, find it difficult to concentrate, I'm sure that children
find it ten if not a hundred times as hard!

Years ago, as a member of a youth club, I remember
that when one church leader was praying we only listened to
count how many times he said the word 'Father' in his prayer. We
were certainly an irreverent bunch, but, if you're interested, the
all-time record was 64!

One way to help people concentrate and own
the prayers that are being said is to give them the chance
to join in with a response. The prayers that follow can be read by
a leader with the rest of the group joining in with the response in
italics. Many of the prayers also go a step further and invite
group members not only to join in with a response, but also to
contribute things to pray about. In this way the prayers can
really belong to the group or congregation and not just be
something that is done for them.

19. Opening prayer

'Lord, teach us to pray ...' Luke 11.1

Lord, there are many things we want to thank
you for,
Father God, help us to pray.
There are many things we want to praise you for,
Father God, help us to pray.
There are many things we want to say sorry for,
Father God, help us to pray.
There are many things we want to ask you for,
Father God, help us to pray.
Lord, as we spend time with you now,
Father God, help us to pray.

20. For a new term

*'He gives me new strength. He guides me in the right
paths as he has promised.' Psalm 23:3*

As we go back to school,
Be with us this term, Lord.
As we learn new things,
Be with us this term, Lord.
As we meet old friends and new,
Be with us this term, Lord.
As we work and play,
Be with us this term, Lord.
In everything we do,
Be with us this term, Lord.

21. For good things to eat

*'He gives food to every living creature; his love is
eternal.' Psalm 136:25*

For cream and butter, eggs and cheese,
Onions, parsnips and green peas
We say … thank you, Lord.
For oranges, bananas and other fresh fruit,
Carrots, cabbage and rosy beetroot
We say … thank you, Lord.
For chewy sweets and sticky toffee,
Cups of tea and mugs of coffee
We say … thank you, Lord.
For chocolate biscuits and birthday cake,
Fizzy drinks and thick milkshakes
We say … thank you, Lord.
For porridge, cornflakes and buttered toast,
Summer picnics and Sunday roast
We say … thank you, Lord.
For hamburgers and spaghetti bolognese,
Tomato ketchup and creamy mayonnaise
We say … thank you, Lord.
For fruit and veg, fish and meat,
For all the good things we like to eat
We say … thank you, Lord.

22. Favourite foods

'What a rich harvest your goodness provides!'
Psalm 65:11

Have ready a large sheet of paper or an OHP acetate plus a selection of coloured pens. Ask the group to name their favourite foods and write down their answers. Alternatively, for added fun, draw their answers! When everyone has been asked, weave all the answers into a response prayer something like this:

For bacon and fried eggs, we really want to say …
Thank you, Lord.
For chicken and pork chops, we really want
    to say …
Thank you, Lord.
For carrots and roast parsnips, we really
    want to say …
Thank you, Lord.
For chocolate cake and sweets, we really want
    to say …
Thank you, Lord.
For cornflakes and salt and vinegar crisps … etc.

23. Action prayer

'...walking and jumping and praising God.' Acts 3:8

Help youngsters to rejoice in the movements of their body by fitting appropriate actions to this prayer. Encourage the children to join in loudly with the response *'Thank you, Lord'*.

> For arms that swing and hands that clap,
> *Thank you, Lord.*
> For feet that stamp and toes that tap,
> *Thank you, Lord.*
> For legs that jump and run and walk,
> *Thank you, Lord.*
> For heads that nod and mouths that talk,
> *Thank you, Lord.*
> Because we can crouch down low, then jump up
>   high,
> *Thank you, Lord.*
> Because we can stand on tip-toe and reach for the
>   sky,
> *Thank you, Lord.*
> For giving us bodies that bend and stretch
>   and move,
> *Thank you, Lord.*

24. For all the things we like to see

'Jesus had pity on them and touched their eyes;
at once they were able to see, and they followed him.'
Matthew 20:34

For the splendour of the sky at daybreak,
Sunlight, raindrops and delicate snowflakes,
For all the things we like to see, thank you, Lord.
For flowering shrubs and green leafy trees,
Sandy beaches and rolling seas,
For all the things we like to see, thank you, Lord.
For stately homes and fairytale castles,
Party decorations and gift-wrapped parcels,
For all the things we like to see, thank you, Lord.
For splendid cities and picturesque villages,
Fresh painted houses and cosy thatched cottages,
For all the things we like to see, thank you, Lord.
For flickering flames and sparkling fireworks,
Pictures, portraits and all kinds of artwork,
For all the things we like to see, thank you, Lord.
For the gift of eyes to see the beauty of the world
around us, thank you, Lord.

25. For ears that hear

'Some people brought him a man who was deaf and could hardly speak and they begged Jesus to place his hands on him.' Mark 7:32

Ask each member of the group to name their favourite noise or sound and list them on a sheet of paper. Weave all the answers into a response prayer something like this:

For birds that sing and friends that chatter,
For fireworks that go whizz and bang,
Thank you, Lord, for ears that hear.
For favourite pop groups and brass bands,
For symphony orchestras and radio programmes,
Thank you, Lord, for ears that hear.
For telephone bells and car horns,
For waterfalls and bird song,
Thank you, Lord ...

26. We are sorry

'Repent, then, and turn to God, so that he will forgive your sins.' Acts 3:19

Explain to your group that, as you read this prayer, you want them to join in with the words *'We are sorry'*, if they agree with what you are saying.

Lord God,
For the times when we think we are better than
    others,
We are sorry.
For the times we have told lies,
We are sorry.
For the times we have joined in with others who are
    doing wrong,
We are sorry.
For the times we have shouted at our friends and
    family,
We are sorry.
For the times when we have refused to apologise,
We are sorry.
For the times when we've ganged up against others,
We are sorry.
For the times when we were too busy with our own
    affairs to notice that other people needed help,
We are sorry.
For these and all our other wrongs,
We are sorry. Amen.

(Fiona Walton)

27. Please help us, Lord.

'Do not conform yourselves to the standards of this world, but let God transform you inwardly by a complete change of your mind. Then you will be able to know the will of God – what is good and is pleasing to him and is perfect.' Romans 12:2

Dear God, we know that there are things about us
    that are not right.
Please help us, Lord.
Sometimes we get angry when we shouldn't.
Please help us, Lord.
Sometimes we are unkind and tease others.
Please help us, Lord.
Sometimes we are selfish and greedy.
Please help us, Lord.
We want to be more like Jesus.
Please help us, Lord.
Thank you that you can help us change.
Please help us, Lord. Amen.

(Sheila Hopkins)

28. Advent prayer

'Prepare a road for the Lord.' Matthew 3:3

In the weeks leading up to Christmas, preparations for December 25th can often take over and it's easy to forget the true reason for all our celebrations.

Lord Jesus, as we buy our Christmas presents,
Help us to remember that we're celebrating your birthday.
As we write our Christmas cards,
Help us to remember that we're celebrating your birthday.
As we put up Christmas decorations,
Help us to remember that we're celebrating your birthday.
As we sing carols,
Help us to remember that we're celebrating your birthday.
As we prepare to celebrate Christmas,
Help us to remember that we're celebrating your birthday.

29. Christmas prayer

'This very day in David's town your Saviour was born –
Christ the Lord!' Luke 2:11

Ask your group to tell you all the things they like best
about Christmas. Write or draw their ideas on a board
or overhead projector acetate. Split the list into groups
of two or three which can be slotted into the following
response prayer:

> Father God, thank you for Christmas cards and
> presents,
> *But most of all, thank you for Jesus.*
> Thank you for Christmas trees and fairy lights,
> *But most of all, thank you for Jesus.*
> Thank you for parties and special outings,
> *But most of all, thank you for Jesus.*
> Thank you for turkey and mince pies,
> *But most of all, thank you for Jesus.*
> Thank you for carol singing and ... etc.

(Evelyn Stewart)

30. For harvest time

'What a rich harvest your goodness provides.'
Psalm 65:11

Bring in three or four packets and tins of food and give
them out to the members of your group. Ask a few
questions to draw out how each product first started its
life and what happened to it en route to the kitchen
cupboard. Make a list of all the stages involved in the
production of, for example, a packet of cornflakes.
Then, use all the ideas to write a response prayer
something like this:

> For the seeds that grow into food crops,
> *Thanks be to God.*
> For the earth where these crops grow,
> *Thanks be to God.*
> For the rain which gently waters them,
> *Thanks be to God.*
> For the farmers that tend and harvest them,
> *Thanks be to God.*
> For the people who process and package our food,
> *Thanks be to God.*
> For the drivers who bring the food to our shops,
> *Thanks be to God.*
> For the shopkeepers who sell us the food,
> *Thanks be to God.*
> For those who buy and cook our food,
> *Thanks be to God.*
> But above all, for that first tiny seed,
> *Thanks be to God.*

31. For a Sunday Club anniversary

'I remember the days gone by, I think about all you have done.' Psalm 143:5

For all the fun we've shared together in the past
    year,
We say ... *Thank you, Lord.*
For all the Bible stories we've heard in the past
    year,
We say ... *Thank you, Lord.*
For all the activities we've enjoyed in the past year,
We say ... *Thank you, Lord.*
For all the new friends we've made in the past year,
We say ... *Thank you, Lord.*
For our (name) ... group and all the things we've
    done together in the past year,
We say ... *Thank you, Lord.*

32. The Bible

*'Your word is a lamp to guide me
and a light for my path.' Psalm 119:105*

The Bible includes stories and records from history
which tell us about your people.
Thank you, Lord, for your special book.
The Bible includes rules which show us how to live
happy lives.
Thank you, Lord, for your special book.
The Bible includes songs and poems which help us
express our feelings to you.
Thank you, Lord, for your special book.
The Bible includes prophecies which contain your
messages for your people.
Thank you, Lord, for your special book.
The Bible includes stories about Jesus which teach
us about your love for us.
Thank you, Lord, for your special book.
The Bible includes letters which give us help,
advice and encouragement.
Thank you, Lord, for your special book.
The Bible is your word for your people.
Thank you, Lord, for your special book.

33. A prayer for peace

'And God's peace which is far beyond human understanding will keep your hearts and minds safe in union with Christ Jesus.' Philippians 4:7

Father God, please take from us our feelings of
frustration
And give us your peace, Lord.
Please take from us all impatient thoughts
And give us your peace, Lord.
Please take from us all feelings of anger and hatred
And give us your peace, Lord.
Please take from us all feelings of greed
And give us your peace, Lord.
Please take from us all selfish and unkind thoughts
And give us your peace, Lord.
Father God, please give us patient and peaceful
hearts.
Please help us to rely on you at all times. Amen
(Fiona Walton)

34. Please, Lord, help us to make peace.

'Turn away from evil and do good;
strive for peace with all your heart.' Psalm 34:14

When we spoil each other's games,
When we call our friends rude names,
Please, Lord, help us to make peace.

When we quarrel, when we fight,
Help us then to put things right,
Please, Lord, help us to make peace.

When we see that things aren't fair,
Help us then to care and share,
Please, Lord, help us to make peace.

(Joan Walker)

35. Inviting Jesus into our lives

'And I pray that Christ will make his home in your hearts through faith.' Ephesians 3:17

Jesus born in a borrowed room,
Make your home in my life.
Jesus, traveller through Judaea,
Make your home in my life.
Jesus, with nowhere to lie down and rest,
Make your home in my life.
Jesus, chased from some towns, welcomed in
others,
Make your home in my life.
Jesus, laid in a borrowed tomb,
Make your home in my life.
Jesus, risen and ascended to heaven,
Make your home in my life.
Jesus, welcome - friend and Lord!
Make your home in my life. Amen.

(Peter Graystone)

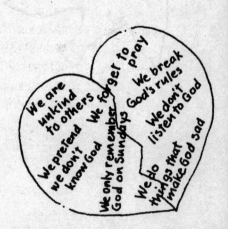

36. Thanking God for his incredible love

'I will bring my people back to me. I will love them with all my heart ...' Hosea 14:4

Ask the group if they can give you suggestions of how we sometimes forget or turn away from God. Write up all these suggestions on a large paper heart (see illustration on facing page).

Explain that this kind of behaviour makes God feel very sad (broken hearted). Cut a large zig zag line through the centre of the heart. However, because God loves us so much he is willing to forgive all the wrong things we have done and give us a fresh start. Turn over the two sides of your paper heart and put them back together clean side uppermost.

Conclude with a prayer thanking God that he still loves us even though we so often turn away from him. For example:

> Father, sometimes we do things that make you sad.
> *Thank you that you still love us.*
> Sometimes we forget to pray.
> *Thank you that you still love us.*
> Sometimes we don't listen to you.
> *Thank you that you still love us.*
> Sometimes we turn away from you.
> *Thank you that you still love us.*
> Father we're sorry for all the times that we've made you sad and hurt you.
> *Thank you for your incredible, never-ending love.*
> Amen.

(Geraldine Witcher)

37. Trusting in God

'Trust in the Lord with all your heart.' Proverbs 3:5

Make a list with your group of all the times when it is good to know that we can trust God to be with us and help us. Weave all the suggestions into a response prayer.

Thank you, Father, that when we are nervous or
    afraid …
We can trust in you.
Thank you that when we have a difficult decision
    to make …
We can trust in you.
Thank you that when we are in an awkward
    situation …
We can trust in you.
Thank you that when we are in trouble …
We can trust in you.
Thank you that when there is no one else
    to turn to …
We can trust in you.
Thank you that whatever we are doing, when we
    need help …
We can trust in you.
Thank you, Lord, that we can depend on you,
    because you never let anyone down. Amen.

(Sheila Hopkins)

38. The one, true God

'We know that there is only the one God.'
1 Corinthians 8:4

Make a list with your group of some of the things
which happened to Jesus, or which Jesus did, during
his life on earth. Use this list to make a response
prayer.

Jesus, born in a stable.
We know that you are the one, true God.
Jesus, who worked as a carpenter.
We know that you are the one, true God.
Jesus, who ate and drank with his friends.
We know that you are the one, true God.
Jesus, who healed the sick.
We know that you are the one, true God.
Jesus, who fed the hungry.
We know that you are the one, true God.
Jesus, who was tempted as we are.
We know that you are the one, true God.
Jesus, who was crucified for us.
We know that you are the one, true God.
Jesus, who was raised from the dead.
We know that you are the one, true God.

(Fiona Walton)

39. Thank you, Lord, for this fine day

'Every day I will thank you; I will praise you for ever and ever.' Psalm 145:2

The song *'Thank you Lord for this fine day'* (Diane Davis Andrews © Celebration/Thankyou Music *Junior Praise* No. 232 published by Marshall Pickering or *Praise God Together* No. 132 published by Scripture Union) can be sung softly as a thoughtful prayer or loudly as a joyful prayer. For special occasions why not invite your group to make up extra verses, eg 'Thank you, Lord, for Mother's Day', 'Thank you, Lord, for Tim's birthday', 'Thank you, Lord, for holiday club' or 'Thank you, Lord, for harvest time'. Alternatively allow group members to suggest lines which include the special things which they would like to thank God for, eg 'Thank you, Lord, for fish and chips' or 'Thank you, Lord, for swimming pools'.

40. One-line prayers

'When you pray do not use a lot of meaningless words, as the pagans do, who think that God will hear them because their prayers are long.' Matthew 6:5

Many adults and children find it hard to pray aloud spontaneously. Very often they are put off by the length of other people's prayers! Have a short time of open prayer in which no one is allowed to contribute anything longer than a one-sentence prayer. However, do not limit the number of times people can join in! With young children you might also want to suggest the first phrase of the prayer, for example:

> *'Father God, we really want to thank you for ...'*

41. The Grace

'May the grace of our Lord Jesus Christ be with you all.' Galatians 6:18

In many churches today the whole congregation repeats the words of The Grace together. To help youngsters feel comfortable at this point in the service it is a good idea to teach them this prayer and to check that they understand the meaning behind it. Suggest that they say this prayer to one another with their eyes open.

> *May the grace of our Lord Jesus Christ and the love of God and the fellowship of the Holy Spirit be with us all ever more. Amen.*

42. Psalm 136

'Give thanks to the Lord, because he is good;
his love is eternal.'

The first nine verses of Psalm 136, plus the last verse,
have been adapted for the following response prayer.

Give thanks to the Lord because he is good;
His love is eternal.
Give thanks to the greatest of all gods;
His love is eternal.
Give thanks to the mightiest of all lords;
His love is eternal.
He alone performs great miracles;
His love is eternal.
By his wisdom he made the heavens;
His love is eternal.
He built the earth on the deep waters;
His love is eternal.
He made the sun and the moon;
His love is eternal.
He gave us the sun to rule over the day;
His love is eternal.
He gave us the moon and the stars to rule over the
    night;
His love is eternal.
Give thanks to the God of heaven;
His love is eternal.

43. Psalm 139

'Lord you have examined me and you know me. You know everything I do; from far away you understand all my thoughts.' Psalm 139:1 and 2

The following response prayer has been based on the words of Psalm 139.

Lord, you know all about me
And you know everything I do.
Thank you, Father, that you know and love me.
You understand all my thoughts.
Thank you, Father, that you know and love me.
You see me when I am working and when I am
    resting.
Thank you, Father, that you know and love me.
Even before I speak, you know what I will say.
Thank you, Father, that you know and love me.
You surround me with your protection and power.
Thank you, Father, that you know and love me.
You created every part of me, you put me together
    in my mother's womb.
Thank you, Father, that you know and love me.
You knew me even before I was born.
Thank you, Father, that you know and love me.
You make me feel unique and special and
    important.
Thank you, Father, that you know and love me.

44. Thank you, Holy Spirit

'For the Spirit that God has given us does not make us timid; instead, his Spirit fills us with power, love and self control.' 2 Timothy 1:7

Thank you, God, for power to praise you.
Thank you, Holy Spirit.
Thank you, God, for power to serve you.
Thank you, Holy Spirit.

Thank you, Lord, for peace and patience.
Thank you, Holy Spirit.
Thank you, Lord, for your dear presence.
Thank you, Holy Spirit.

Thank you, God, for acts of healing.
Thank you, Holy Spirit.
Thank you, God, for true believing.
Thank you, Holy Spirit.

Thank you, Lord, for faith to trust you.
Thank you, Holy Spirit.
Thank you, Lord, for power to love you.
Thank you, Holy Spirit.

Thank you, God, for courage and boldness.
Thank you, Holy Spirit.
Thank you, God, for all your greatness.
Thank you, Holy Spirit.

(Geraldine Witcher)

45. Three-part prayer

Ask a leader to read the lines marked 1, and divide the
rest of the group into two sections to read the lines
marked 2 and 3. Practise the responses with each group
beforehand and check that they know when to join in.

1. For the good things that have happened
    this week,
2. Thank you, Lord Jesus
3. And praise you, Son of God.
1. For all our friends and family,
2. Thank you, Lord Jesus
3. And praise you, Son of God.
1. For all your love and care for us,
2. Thank you, Lord Jesus
3. And praise you, Son of God.
1. For always being there for us,
2. Thank you, Lord Jesus
3. And praise you, Son of God.
1. For choosing us to be your friends,
2. Thank you, Lord Jesus
3. And praise you, Son of God.
All: Amen.

46. Making time for God

'Martha was upset over all the work she had to do, so she came and said, "Lord, don't you care that my sister has left me to do all the work by myself? Tell her to come and help me!"

'The Lord answered her, "Martha, Martha! You are worried and troubled over so many things, but just one is needed. Mary has chosen the right thing and it will not be taken from her."' Luke 10:40 and 41

When we're busy with lots to do,
Help us, Lord, to make time for you.
When we're happy and having fun,
Help us, Lord, to make time for you.
When we're lonely, frightened or sad,
Help us, Lord, to make time for you.
Wherever we are, at home or at school,
Help us, Lord, to make time for you.
Thank you, Lord, that you always have time for us,
Help us, Lord, to make time for you.

(Geraldine Witcher)

47. Lord, help me to depend on you

'I depend on God alone; I put my hope in him.'
Psalm 62:5

When I'm in a difficult situation,
Lord, help me to depend on you.
When I'm tempted to do things in my own strength,
Lord, help me to depend on you.
When I'm worried and I don't know what to do,
Lord, help me to depend on you.
When I have a difficult decision to make,
Lord, help me to depend on you.
In every part of my life,
Lord, help me to depend on you. Amen.

48. Our God reigns

'Your Kingdom, O God, will last for ever and ever!'
Hebrews 1:8

Each month of every year
Our God reigns!
Each week of every month
Our God reigns!
Each day of every month
Our God reigns!
Each hour of every day
Our God reigns!
Each moment in time
Our God relgns!
Be still and in this moment
Know that our God relgns.

49. Help us to forgive

'Forgive us the wrongs we have done, as we forgive the wrongs that others have done to us.' Matthew 6:12

Father God, when someone does something
   to upset us,
Help us to forgive.
When someone breaks friends with us,
Help us to forgive.
When our feelings have been hurt,
Help us to forgive.
When we have been hit and feel like crying,
Help us to forgive.
When someone tells lies about us,
Help us to forgive.
Thank you Lord that you are always willing to
   forgive us, help us to be ready to forgive others
   when they wrong us. Amen.

(Clive de Salis)

50. Through the window

'In an upstairs room of his house there were windows that faced towards Jerusalem. There, just as he had always done, he (Daniel) knelt down at the open windows and prayed to God three times a day.'
Daniel 6:10

Daniel evidently found it helpful to pray beside an open window. Take your group to stand by a window and ask them to list all the things that they can see and would like to thank God for. Invite everyone to pray short one-line prayers or ask a leader to weave all the suggestions into one concluding prayer.

51. For holidays

'He lets me rest in fields of green grass and leads me to quiet pools of fresh water.' Psalm 23:2

At the end of a school term many children want to thank God for the holidays. Ask your group to list all the reasons that they enjoy the holidays and then weave all of their suggestions into a response prayer something like this:

> Holidays give us time to rest and relax,
> So we say ... *Thank you, Father God.*
> Holidays give us time to spend with family and
>   friends,
> So we say ... *Thank you, Father God.*
> Holidays give us time for fun and games,

So we say ... *Thank you, Father God.*
Holidays give us time to read new books,
So we say ... *Thank you, Father God.*
Holidays give us time to visit new places,
So we say ... *Thank you, Father God.*

52. Closing prayer
'Lord, hear my prayer!' Psalm 143:1

Lord, for all the things we have thanked you for
Hear our prayers, Father God.
For all the things we have praised you for
Hear our prayers, Father God.
For all the things we have asked you for
Hear our prayers, Father God.
For all the things we have said sorry for
Hear our prayers, Father God.
For all the concerns we have shared with you
Hear our prayers, Father God.

Section Three

PRAYERS TO SHOUT OUT LOUD

As children we used to impersonate
the stereotype vicar who would adopt a special voice for
Sundays and recite the prayers in an affected voice. It seemed to
us that you couldn't talk to God in everyday tones, but had to use
long words and a solemn, sonorous voice. It's important that
youngsters today know that they can talk to God in their normal
voices. They don't have to use long words or set phrases, but can
talk to God as they would to a friend. Sometimes they might want
to pray silently in their heads, sometimes they might want to
pray out loud, but softly, and on other occasions they might want
to shout their prayers at the top of their voices.

Jesus was pleased when he heard the children shouting
in the Temple, 'Praise to David's Son!' (Matthew 21:15) The chief
priests and the teachers of the Law were annoyed, but Jesus
called their shouts 'perfect praise' (Matthew 21:16). The Psalms
also teach us that it is good to shout our thanks and praise to
God. You only have to read some of the verses chosen to
accompany the following prayers.

53. A loud 'Thank you!'

'I will give loud thanks to the Lord,' Psalm 109:30

Ask the group to look back over the previous week and think about some of the things they would like to thank God for. Weave all of their suggestions into a response prayer with the children joining in with the response loudly and clearly. For example:

> For all the new things we've learnt this week, we really want to shout…
> *Thank you, Lord!*
> For all the good food we've enjoyed this week, we really want to shout…
> *Thank you, Lord!*
> For all the fun games we've played this week, we really want to shout…
> *Thank you, Lord!*
> For all the great TV programmes we've watched this week, we really want to shout…
> *Thank you, Lord!*
> For all the friends we've spent time with this week, we really want to shout…
> *Thank you, Lord!*

54. A shout of praise

'Praise God with shouts of joy, all people!' Psalm 66:1

Leader: Who is with us day by day?
All: Jesus!
Leader: Who can show us what to say?
All: Jesus!
Leader: When we're weak, then who is strong?
All: Jesus!
Leader: Who can forgive us for doing wrong?
All: Jesus!
Leader: Who is great, all others above?
All: Jesus!
Leader: Who surrounds us with his love?
All: Jesus!
Leader: Who is stronger than the crowd?
All: Jesus!
Leader: Who do we want to praise out loud?
All: Jesus!

(Bill Paice)

55. Who do we appreciate?

'Blow trumpets and horns, and shout for joy to the Lord,'
Psalm 98:6

Youngsters are used to showing their appreciation for a football team with loud enthusiasm, so why should they keep quiet about their love for Jesus? Divide your group in two to shout the following chant. This chant can work particularly well at a holiday club or similar children's event.

1: 2, 4, 6, 8!
2: Who do we appreciate?
1 and 2: JESUS!
1: J.E.S.U.S.
2: Yes!
1 and 2: JESUS!

56. Who's the best?

'Shout the news gladly; make it known everywhere,'
Isaiah 48:20

Leader: Who's the best?
Group: Jesus!
Leader: J.E.S.U.S.
Group: Yes!
Leader: Shout his name from East to West!
Group: Jesus!
All: He's the best!

57. International praise

'Praise the Lord all nations!' Psalm 117:1

There are thousands and thousands of Christians all around the world, so why not teach your group to shout 'Praise the Lord!' in a different language?

> **German:** Lob den Herrn!
> **Dutch:** Looft den Here!
> **French:** Le Seigneur soit loué!
> **Hebrew:** Hallelu jah!
> **Spanish:** El Señor sea glorificado!
> **Italian:** Il Signore sia lodato!

Divide your group into smaller sections and ask each one to practise the words 'Praise the Lord!' in a different language. Have someone stand at the front, rather like a conductor, and point at the groups when they should shout out their words. Let the groups take part in turn, sometimes together and sometimes on their own.

Why not give out large sticky labels and let your group write 'Praise the Lord!' on their label in the language of their choice? If the group wear the labels on their clothing throughout the day they will have the opportunity of telling other people what it means.

58. Prayer chant

'God has given us eternal life, and this life has its source in his Son.' 1 John 5:11

Ask your group to make a list of the things which they treasure. Use their ideas to make a prayer chant as follows:

1: My bike is precious,
All: But it won't last for ever.
2: The television is precious,
All: But it won't last for ever.
3: A watch is precious,
All: But it won't last for ever.
4: My computer is precious,
All: But it won't last for ever.

Finish with the following lines:

Leader: God's gift of eternal life is precious …
All: And it will last for ever! Hallelujah! Thank you, Lord!

(Sheila Hopkins)

59. A shout of belief

'And how can they believe if they have not heard the message? And how can they hear if the message is not proclaimed?' Romans 10:14

Teach your group the following acclamation of our belief in Jesus Christ. Repeat the words several times starting softly and rising to a loud and joyful crescendo. Introduce the acclamation each time with the question 'What do we believe?'

Christ has died
Christ is risen
Christ will come again
Hallelujah!

60. Jesus is special!
'May your people shout for joy!' Psalm 132:9

The following shout of praise works well with large groups of children. Encourage the youngsters to shout out the words and letters loudly and clearly.

S.P.E.C.I.A.L.
Jesus is SPECIAL
Let's shout and yell,
S.P.E.C.I.A.L.
We praise you Jesus,
We'll go and tell.
S.P.E.C.I.A.L.
He's our friend,
He's SPECIAL!

(Eileen Turner)

61. There's no need to be afraid

'When I am afraid, O Lord Almighty, I put my trust in you.' Psalm 56:3

In this prayer the group should shout out the response loudly and confidently.

Leader: There's no need to be afraid. Why not?
Group: Because Jesus is with us!
Leader: There's no need to be dismayed. Why not?
Group: Because Jesus is with us!
Leader: There's no need to feel scared. Why not?
Group: Because Jesus is with us!
Leader: There's no need to feel frightened.
    Why not?
Group: Because Jesus is with us!
Leader: There's no need to feel worried. Why not?
Group: Because Jesus is with us!
Leader: So we'll trust in him and be at peace,
Group: Because Jesus is with us!

62. God's creation

'Praise the Lord God of Israel, Creator of heaven and earth!' 2 Chronicles 2:12

The following questions and answers work well when they are shouted loudly and clearly. A leader should ask the questions and the group shouts out the response given in italics.

Who created the bright sunlight?
Who created the stars at night?
Our Father God - That's who!
Who created the moon and stars?
Who created Jupiter and Mars?
Our Father God - That's who!
Who created the rolling seas?
Who created shady trees?
Our Father God - That's who!
Who created the clouds in the sky?
Who created birds that fly?
Our Father God - That's who!
Who created storms and showers?
Who created plants and flowers?
Our Father God - That's who!
Who created everything we see?
Who created you and me?
Our Father God - That's who!

63. Clap the rhythm

'How wonderful are your gifts to me; how good they are!'
Psalm 16:6

Stand in a circle and give each group member a few
moments to think of one thing that he or she does well.
Explain that you are going to ask the group to call out
the things that they can do as part of a prayer chant
thanking God for all the things we can do. The lines of
the prayer are followed by a clapping rhythm of two
slow beats (clap…clap) followed by three faster beats
(clap…clap…clap). Everyone says the 'Praise God' part
together then a leader should point at someone to add
the 'I can…' line. For example:

> **All:** Praise God! (clap…clap)
> **Child 1:** I can draw. (clap…clap…clap)
> **All:** Praise God! (clap…clap)
> **Child 2:** I can dance. (clap…clap…clap)
> **All:** Praise God! (clap…clap)
> **Child 3:** I can ride. (clap…clap…clap)
> **All:** Praise God! (clap…clap)
> **Child 4:** I can play football. (clap…clap…clap)
> **All:** Praise God! (clap…clap)
> **Child 5:** I can tell jokes. (clap…clap…clap)
> **All:** Praise God! (clap…clap)

(Marina Brown)

64. Parachute praise

'I will give you thanks as long as I live; I will raise my hands to you in prayer.' Psalm 63:4

Many churches and holiday club groups borrow a parachute or play canopy from time to time to use as part of a games session. A parachute can also be incorporated into your time of praise and prayer. You might like to spread the parachute on the floor and let each group member sit on the edge of the parachute. You can then use any of the response prayers from the section 'Prayers to join in' with the parachute, contributing to the general feeling of group identity and oneness. Invite the group to pray short one-line prayers around the circle, or to pray for those sitting opposite or on either side of them.

Alternatively, invite the group to stand up and hold on to the edge of the parachute with both hands. To a count of four slowly waft the parachute up and down (up 1, 2, down 3, 4). When everyone has grown accustomed to the rhythm a leader can then encourage the group to join in with a response prayer thanking God for all the good things that have happened during

the Sunday Club or Holiday Club. The leader should speak as the parachute is coming down and the group shouts out the response 'Lord, we lift our thanks to you!' as the parachute is being wafted up again.

For the fun and games that we've enjoyed today,
Lord, we lift our thanks to you!
For the music and singing,
Lord, we lift our thanks to you!
For the stories we've heard,
Lord, we lift our thanks to you!
For art and craft,
Lord, we lift our thanks to you!
For the new friends we've made,
Lord, we lift our thanks to you!

65. Praise poem
'And I will be with you always, to the end of the age.'
Matthew 28:20

The following poem begins quite quietly, but rises to a loud crescendo at the end.

In sad times,
In bad times,
In worry and confusion - Jesus is beside me.
In good times,
In great times,
In joy and excitement - Jesus is beside me.
Jesus is alive and here with me - NOW!
(All cheer!)

(Marina Brown)

Section Four

PRAYERS TO WRITE, DRAW AND MAKE

Prayers don't have to be said,
we can also respond to God creatively by drawing or
writing our thoughts. You've probably heard the saying 'a picture
speaks a thousand words' which is certainly true of great
artwork. As I write this paragraph I am looking at a picture of a
waterfall drawn by Joni Eareckson Tada. Every pencil mark
contributes to praise God for the beauty of his creation.

You don't need to be a great artist to draw a picture
that will please God, any more than you need to be a great orator
to pray in words. Sometimes taking the time to draw, for example,
something we want to thank God for, can make us stop, think and
take a little more time and care over our prayer. For the same
reasons, writing a prayer can also be helpful. It is sometimes a
good idea to let people choose whether they write or draw their
prayer, since this enables them to choose the medium with which
they feel more comfortable.

Often the pictures and written prayers can be
displayed for the benefit and enrichment of everyone who
sees them and in this way they also serve as a lasting
reminder of the original prayer.

66. Gift of praise

'Now, our God, we give you thanks, and we praise your glorious name.' 1 Chronicles 29:13

Make a gift of praise for God. Gift wrap a small cardboard box and tie a bright ribbon around it, or paste a large square of gift wrap onto backing paper and add ribbons so that it looks like a present. Then, give out small pieces of paper or sticky labels and ask the group to each draw or write something that they want to thank God for. Play some quiet music while people come up one at a time to paste or stick their prayers on to the box.

67. News collage

'First of all, then, I urge that petitions, prayers, requests and thanksgivings be offered to God for all people ...'
1 Timothy 2:1

It is important that our prayers are relevant and topical. Why not bring in two or three local and national newspapers and invite your group to cut out pictures and headlines concerning issues that they would like to pray about. Use all these cuttings to make a collage that will be a stimulus for open prayer. When you have finished, display the collage on the wall under the caption, 'Father God, we pray for …' In this way the collage will remind people to continue praying for the topics shown.

68. Praise offering

'Let us, then, always offer praise to God as our sacrifice through Jesus, which is the offering presented by lips that confess him as Lord.' Hebrews 13:15

If your church takes up an offering each week, why not use this as an opportunity to also give God an offering of praise. Give out small slips of paper and invite people to write or draw something that they want to praise or thank God for. When the offering plate is passed around, invite people to put in both their money and their offering of praise.

69. Prayer flower

'Long ago you created the earth, and with your own hands you made the heavens.' Psalm 102:25

Cut out a large circle to represent the centre of a flower and write on it the words 'Praise God for…'. Cut out a petal shape for each member of your group and invite them to write on it some aspect of creation for which they would like to thank God. For example: sunshine, horses, oak trees, sandy beaches, rainbows. Arrange the petals around the edge of the circle to look like a flower and mount all the pieces on backing paper (see illustration). Have a few moments of silence in which you can dedicate your prayers to God.

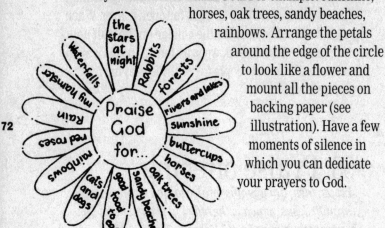

70. Prayer paper chain

'Be joyful always, pray at all times, be thankful in all circumstances.' 1 Thessalonians 5:16-18

Give each member of the group a strip of coloured paper and encourage them to write a one-line thank you prayer. Fasten all the strips together to make a festive paper chain that you can hang across your meeting room. If you only have a small group you might want to give each person two or three strips of paper or add to the chain week by week. The prayer paper chain is particularly effective on special occasions like Christmas, Easter and church anniversaries when a long chain can be made during an all-age service.

71. Christmas stars

'Let us thank God for his priceless gift.'
2 Corinthians 9:15

Use the star shape illustrated to make several
cardboard templates. Have ready some sheets of thin
card so that each member of the group can draw round
a template and cut out their own star. Then, invite your
group to write one-line prayers thanking God for the
gift of his own Son on that first Christmas. Decorate
the edges of the prayer stars with glitter, then punch a
hole in the top of each one and attach a piece of ribbon,
so that they can be hung on a Christmas tree. If your
church has its own tree, why not encourage group
members to make two decorations: one to take home
and one for the church tree. These prayer stars are far
more in keeping with the true meaning of Christmas
than plastic Father Christmases and snowmen on skis!

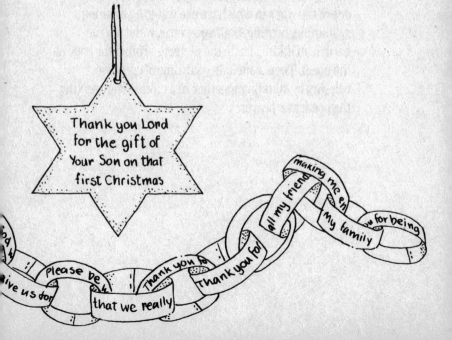

72. Thank you, Lord, for water

'Worship him who made heaven, earth, sea, and the springs of water!' Revelation 14:7

On a large sheet of paper write out the following poem:

> Thank you, Lord, for giving us water,
> Cold and salty in the clear blue sea.
> Hot and bubbly in the bath at night,
> Pure and healthy from the tap for me.
> As I wash my hands until they're clean,
> I remember your love washes badness away,
> Thank you, Lord, for loving me.
> (Joan Walker)

Give each member of the group a raindrop-shaped piece of paper and ask them to draw a picture showing one of the ways in which we use water, eg washing, swimming, boating, boiling a kettle, watering the garden, drinking. Paste the pictures around the edge of the poem. Then, conclude your time of creative worship by standing together in a circle and repeating the poem as a prayer.

73. Prayer bricks

'Finally, build up your strength in union with the Lord and by means of his mighty power.' Ephesians 6:10

Make the point that a strong church is a church that prays together for its work and for its members. Draw an outline of your church building on a large sheet of paper. Then, give each member of the group a rectangle of paper and ask them to write a prayer for the church, for the church leaders, for one of the organisations attached to the church or for a particular member who is perhaps ill or away. When everyone has finished their 'prayer brick' invite them to come up and paste it on to the outline of the church. You may wish to continue this activity in subsequent weeks until the whole church is covered with prayer bricks.

					Thank you for all you have done here	Please be with the Rev Jones, Lord
					Thank you for this SS Group	Lord, thank you for the church
					Father, you helped me recently	Father, please gee us up
Thank you, Lord for Pathfinders	Thank you for the Brownies	Please make Mr Smith better, Lord		Bless us at Scouts, Lord	Dear Lord, be with the choir, please	Thank you for our love for each other
Help us to care for each other, Lord		Please be with Mrs Dale, Lord		Please watch over our music group	Please be with the curate and his family	Be with us at holiday club
		Please be with the Guides, Lord	Thank you Lord, for Beavers		Please be with the Sunday School	Bless our Youth Club, Lord

74. Hand prayers

'I will raise my hands to you in prayer.' Psalm 63:4

Give each member of your group a piece of paper and ask them to draw round and cut out the shape of their own hand. On the four fingers they should write:

1. something to praise God for,
2. something to thank God for,
3. something for which they would like to ask for God's help,
4. something they would like to say sorry about.

Group members can fold down the fingers on their paper hand if they wish to keep their prayers secret.

A leader should conclude by praying for the group, leaving pauses for people to bring their own prayers to God silently.

75. Praise poster

'My heart praises the Lord; my soul is glad because of God my Saviour...' Luke 1:46 and 47

In small groups read Luke 1:46-55 (Mary's song of praise) and pick out the phrases that describe God. Give each group member a sheet of paper and ask them to write out one of the phrases in large, colourful lettering. Paste all the finished phrases on to backing paper under the caption, 'We can praise God because...'

(Heather Bell)

76. Balloon prayers
'Worship the Lord with joy ...' Psalm 100:2

Have ready a number of inflated balloons and a selection
of permanent marker pens or overhead projector pens.
Ask your group to suggest one-line thank you prayers
and write two or three prayers on each balloon. Hang
the balloons in clusters around your church or meeting
room. Like the prayer paper chains, these balloon
prayers could be made during an all-age service as part
of a special church celebration.

77. Thank you letter
*'Let us praise God for his glorious grace for the free gift he
gave us in his dear Son!' Ephesians 1:6*

After Christmas many people write a thank you letter to
all the people who gave them a gift. Why not write a
huge, group thank you letter to God, thanking him for
his special gift to us at Christmas? Have ready a large
sheet of paper on which you have written the address of
your group, the date and the words 'Dear Father God'
laid out to look like a letter. At the bottom of the letter
write 'With love from us all'. Give out sticky labels and
invite everyone to draw or write their own contribution
to this letter. Younger children might want to draw
something that they have particularly enjoyed about
Christmas, while older folk might want to write a one-
line prayer thanking God for the birth of Jesus.

Ask a few people to collect in all the labels and stick
them on the letter, while the rest of the group sing two or
three songs. Once the letter is complete, a leader should
conclude in prayer, offering the letter to God.

78. New Year

'I will give you a new heart and a new mind.'
Ezekiel 36:26

Give each member of your group a piece of paper and show them how to fold it in half and then tear it into a heart shape. Encourage each group member to write the following words on their heart:

> *Lord, in the year that's about to start,*
> *Help me to love you with all my heart.*

Read out the following prayer and invite group members to read out the words written on their hearts as a response:

> Father God, as we look forward to the coming year,
>   we ask that you will bless us and be close to us.
> *Lord, in the year that's about to start,*
> *Help me to love you with all my heart.*
> Father God, please help us to make the most of all
>   the opportunities that you give us in the next
>   twelve months.
> *Lord, in the year that's about to start,*
> *Help me to love you with all my heart.*
> Father God, please give us the strength and courage
>   to bear the difficulties and disappointments of
>   the coming year.
> *Lord, in the year that's about to start,*
> *Help me to love you with all my heart.*
> Father God, in everything we do this year, may we
>   turn to you for help and guidance.
> *Lord, in the year that's about to start,*
> *Help me to love you with all my heart.*
> Amen.

(Fiona Walton)

79. New Year resolutions

'They went into the house, and when they saw the child with his mother Mary, they knelt down and worshipped him.' Matthew 2:11

Remind your group of the wise men who travelled a long way to find Jesus. When they found him they knelt down and worshipped him and offered him special gifts. What could we resolve to do during this New Year to show Jesus how much he means to us?

Discuss the different possibilities and write up all the suggestions on a board or overhead projector acetate. For example: we could set aside a regular time to talk to God, we could try to read our Bible more often, we could be more willing to share our possessions, we could resolve to tell someone else the good news about Jesus. Conclude with a prayer asking God to help the group keep their New Year's resolutions.

80. Harvest collage

'The fields are covered with sheep; the valleys are full of wheat. Everything shouts and sings for joy.' Psalm 65:13

Spend a little time discussing favourite foods and then give each group member a yellow or orange piece of paper shaped like a grain of wheat (see illustration). Invite everyone to use their paper shape to write a short harvest prayer thanking God for the gift of food. Younger children could perhaps draw their favourite food. Paste these prayers onto a sheet of dark coloured backing paper in groups of seven or nine to look like one or more ears of wheat. Add the caption, 'Thank you, Father God, for the harvest you have provided for us.'

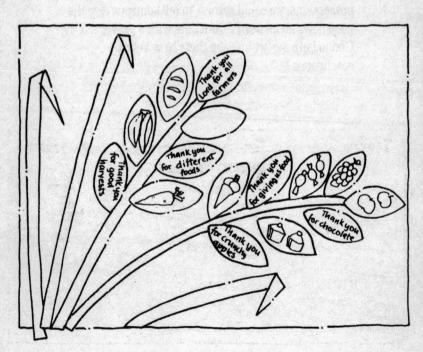

81. Five senses

*'Our Lord and God! You are worthy to receive glory,
honour and power. For you created all things, and by
your will they were given existence and life.'*
Revelation 4:11

Talk about all the many things that God has created
and try to inspire awe and wonder for the size, extent
and beauty of God's creation. Ask your group to think
about all the different things that God has created and
to consider what they most like to touch, taste, smell,
hear or see. Have ready plenty of paper shapes cut to
resemble eyes, ears, noses, lips and hands. Ask your
group to write one or two of their ideas on the
appropriate pieces of paper. Group the shapes together
to form a big praise poster under the title, 'Thank you,
Father, for the wonder of your creation.' (See
illustration.)

Conclude with a prayer thanking God for all the
marvellous things he has created and asking him to
help us care for them wisely.

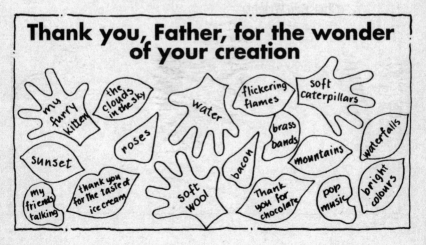

82. Fold a prayer

'First of all then I urge that petitions, prayers, requests and thanksgivings be offered to God for all people...'
1 Timothy 2:1

Give each member of your group a piece of paper and ask them to write a one-line prayer request at the top of the page. When they have done this they should fold over the paper. Everyone should then pass their paper to the person on their left. Each group member should now have a different piece of paper on which they can write another one-line prayer and fold it over. If they wish to they can write the same prayer again. The paper should be passed on several more times until there are five or six prayers on the page, at which point everyone should stop, unfold and read their paper. Invite everyone to spend a few moments silently offering these prayers to God. If you have time, ask everyone to put their papers in a pile in the middle and invite them to take out and read a new set of prayers.

(Christine Wright)

83. For a child's birthday

'But continue to grow in the grace and knowledge of our Lord and Saviour Jesus Christ.' 2 Peter 3:18

When a child in your group has a birthday it is a good idea to make a point of saying a special prayer for them. A leader might read aloud the prayer below or it could be written in a birthday card that the whole group signs.

> Thank you Lord for ....'s birthday. Please give him/her a happy day. Thank you for all the good things that happened last year and please bless him/her, keep him/her safe and help him/her to grow closer to you in the year ahead. Amen.

84. Pop the balloon

'I will forgive their sins and will no longer remember their wrongs.' Hebrews 8:12

Have ready a large inflated balloon and a permanent marker pen. Ask your group to name some of the reasons for which we might need to say sorry to God, for example: telling lies, not being willing to share, being grumpy, swearing, not making time to talk to God. Write all the ideas on your balloon. Then, have a few moments of prayer asking God's forgiveness for all the things we do wrong and including all the suggestions written on the balloon. Finally pop the balloon and explain that when we say sorry to God, he not only forgives us, but he also forgets the wrong things we have done and gives us the chance to make a fresh start.

85. In the bin

'Happy are those whose wrongs are forgiven, whose sins are pardoned! Happy is the person whose sins the Lord will not keep account of!' Romans 4:7 and 8

Give each member of the group a small slip of paper and invite them to write a short prayer saying sorry to God for anything which is on their mind. Have a few moments of silence in which people can quietly offer their prayers to God and then pass round a bin and ask everyone to tear up their prayer and put the pieces in the bin. As with 'Pop the balloon', explain that when we say sorry to God, God takes away all our wrongdoing and gives us the chance to make a fresh start. If you are able to go outside, you might like to put all the torn-up prayers in a metal waste-bin and then set light to them.

86. Forgiven through the cross

'God forgave us all our sins; he cancelled the unfavourable record of our debts with its binding rules and did away with it completely by nailing it to the cross.' Colossians 2:13 and 14

Draw an outline of a cross on a large sheet of a paper. Give each member of the group a piece of paper or, if possible, a yellow Post-It note. Invite the group to write prayers thanking Jesus that through his death on the cross we can be forgiven for all our wrongdoing. Play some quiet music and let people come up one at a time to place their prayers around the cross.

87. Easter prayer

'Let us all give thanks to the God and Father of our Lord Jesus Christ! Because of his great mercy he gave us new life by raising Jesus Christ from death.' 1 Peter 1:3

Give each member of your group a small foil-wrapped Easter egg. Ask them to unwrap the egg carefully, and while they are eating the chocolate to fashion the foil wrapper into a small cross. Explain that at Easter we are celebrating new life. Jesus died on the cross to take the punishment for all the wrong things we have done, but three days later he rose again and he is still alive today. An egg represents the joy of new life – the new life of a baby chicken. It reminds us that Jesus is still alive today and offers new life to all who believe in him.

Pray, thanking God for the symbols of the cross and the egg which help us to remember that because Jesus died on the cross for us, we can have new life in him.

88. Easter mobile

'The Lord will take delight in you and in his love he will give you new life' Zephaniah 3:17

Give each member of the group a cardboard shape of either a rabbit, a chicken or an egg and ask what these three things have to do with Easter. Draw out that all three represent new life: the new life of a baby chicken or rabbit, the promise of new life hidden in the egg. At Easter we exchange chocolate eggs, rabbits and chickens as a symbol of the new life of Jesus. Jesus died on the cross to take the punishment for all the wrong things we have done, but three days later he rose again and he's still alive today. He offers the chance of new life to all who believe and trust in him. Invite each group member to decorate with sticky shapes or colour in their cardboard shape. On the back they could write a prayer praising God that Jesus rose again and is alive today and thanking him for his gift to us of new life.

Punch a hole in the top of each shape, thread a ribbon through the hole and then attach the rabbits, chickens and eggs to a wire coathanger to make an attractive Easter prayer mobile.

Thank you Lord for your gift of new life.

Hallelujah Jesus is alive!

89. Flame prayers

'Then they saw what looked like tongues of fire which spread out and touched each person there.' Acts 2:3

Cut simple flame shapes from yellow, orange and red paper. Give each member of your group a shape and explain to them that when God's Holy Spirit first came it was as if tongues of fire were reaching out and touching all the people. It wasn't the kind of flame that burnt people, but more like a flame that filled people with the warmth and love of God, a flame which fired up their hearts with courage and enthusiasm.

God sent his Holy Spirit to help people live as Christians. Today the Holy Spirit can help people pray and praise. He can help people read and understand the Bible. He can help people tell others about Jesus. God sent us his Holy Spirit to dwell in us and to be our special helper. Encourage everyone to use their flame shapes to write a prayer thanking God for his wonderful gift.

Collect in the finished prayers and paste them on to a dark background to look like one big flame. Explain that as the Holy Spirit helps us to tell more and more people about Jesus, so more and more people can be fired up with the love of God.

90. Jesus, the light of the world

"'I am the light of the world," he said. "Whoever follows me will have the light of life and will never walk in darkness."' John 8:12

Bring in an orange and explain that it represents the world. Talk about some of the countries which people often visit on holiday and the countries where your church has contact with mission partners. You might also like to mention any countries which are currently in the news, perhaps because they are torn apart by war or because they are suffering floods or famine etc. Write the names of these countries on sticky labels, fold the label in half and stick it around a cocktail stick. Then ask one or two volunteers to come out and fix these cocktail stick flags into the orange. Explain that Jesus cares about these countries very much and that Jesus is not just Lord in our country, but in every country. Light a birthday cake candle in a small candle holder and fix this candle into the top of the orange. (You may need to make a small hole in advance.) Explain that Jesus is the light of the world - the light which guides us and leads us out of darkness.

Finish with a prayer asking that God will be very close to those who work at home and abroad telling others about the light of Jesus. Thank God that he cares about those countries that are suffering and ask that the love and light of Jesus might shine in their darkness.

(Hint: If you can manage to find the special relighting candles, you can also make the point that the darkness can never extinguish the light of Jesus. John 1:5)

91. Paper plate grace

'He sat down to eat with them, took the bread and said the blessing ...' Luke 24:30

Younger children might enjoy writing and illustrating a mealtime grace. Give each child a paper plate and let them compose their own grace to write in the centre. Help the children to cut pictures of food from suitable magazines to paste around the edge of the plate. Encourage the youngsters to take their grace home to remind them to thank God for his goodness before they eat a meal.

92. Grace box

'Then he took the five loaves and two fish, looked up to heaven, and gave thanks to God.' Matthew 14:19

If you are taking a group of youngsters on a camp or weekend away, why not take a little time at the beginning of your holiday to sit down with the children and help them all to write a simple grace. Put all these prayers in a small box, for example a card index box, and draw out a different prayer to read before each meal.

93. For our homes

'I know that your goodness and love will be with me all my life; and your house will be my home as long as I live.' Psalm 23:6

Take a sheet of A4 paper and a pair of scissors, then follow the instructions below to cut out first a house, then a door and finally a window. If you want the whole group to be involved give everyone a sheet of paper and encourage them to copy you. If you do not have enough pairs of scissors it is equally possible, and in many ways more fun, to tear the paper. (Hint: It is a good idea to make a fold in the paper where you intend to tear it as this helps to produce a straight tear. Practise beforehand!) Stop after each of the three stages to talk about the shape and then pray as follows ...

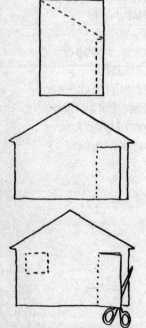

1. **House.** Father God, we want to thank you for our homes. Thank you for the warmth and security they provide. Please help us to make our homes a place where you come first.

2. **Door.** Father God, we pray for visitors to our homes. Help us to make them feel special and welcome. We pray that they will feel your love and peace whenever they visit us.

3. **Window.** When we look out of a window we can see the world around us. Help us to see the needs of others and to be willing to help them.

94. Prayer walk

'How clearly the sky reveals God's glory!' Psalm 19:1

Prayers don't always have to be said indoors with your
eyes firmly closed! Why not take your whole group
outside for a prayer walk. Stop at intervals to look
around and thank God for all the good things that you
can see and to ask for God's help over anything of
concern (eg safety on the road, pollution).

95. Graffiti wall

'Pray always for all God's people.' Ephesians 6:18

Roll out a very long piece of old wallpaper and attach it
horizontally to the wall, reverse side uppermost. Have
ready a selection of marker pens and invite your group
to write down anything they would like to say to God.
They might like to think of two or three things they
would like to thank God for and two or three things for
which they would like to ask for God's help. Encourage
everyone to write all over the paper and not just in one
corner! Then, have a few minutes of silent prayer in
which the group can walk up and down the length of
the graffiti wall, reading each other's prayers and
silently bringing them to God.

96. Snowflakes

'Even the hairs of your head have all been counted.'
Luke 12:7

Give each group member a circle of paper and show them how to fold and cut it to make a snowflake. See illustration below. (Hint: If you do not have enough scissors for the whole group, you might like to try tearing the paper.) When everyone has cut out their own snowflake and unfolded it to reveal the shape, compare all the different patterns. You should find that no two snowflakes are identical. Microscopes reveal that snowflakes are made up of tiny six-sided ice crystals and no two crystals are exactly the same. No two people are identical either. Each person is unique; even twins are really quite different. As a group compose a prayer praising God that each person is special and unique and thanking him that he knows each of us inside out. He even knows how many hairs we have on our head! Write out the prayer, then paste it on to a sheet of black paper with all the snowflakes displayed around the edge.

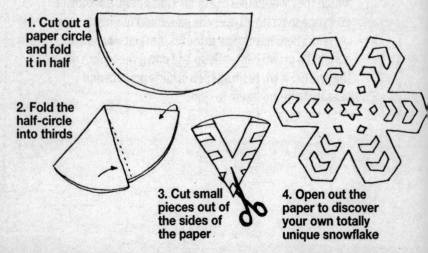

1. Cut out a paper circle and fold it in half

2. Fold the half-circle into thirds

3. Cut small pieces out of the sides of the paper

4. Open out the paper to discover your own totally unique snowflake

97. Hospital prayer

'Is there anyone who is ill? He should send for the church elders, who will pray for him and rub olive oil on him in the name of the Lord.' James 5:14

Draw a simple outline of a hospital building on a large sheet of paper (see illustration). On the left-hand side of the picture make a list of those people known to your group who are involved in caring for the health and well-being of others. On the right-hand side of the picture make a list of those people known to the group who are unwell. Use the picture as a stimulus for prayer thanking God for the skill of those people who care for our health and asking him to be with those who are ill.

98. People who help us

'I always thank my God as I remember you in my prayers.' Philemon 4

The following idea is particularly suitable for younger groups. Give each youngster an A4 piece of paper and show them how to fold it five times, concertina style. Draw a figure on the first fold of paper with its feet and hands touching the outside edges. Then cut round the figure so that the fold remains intact at the feet and hands. When you open out the paper you should have five people standing in a line. On each of the five paper people write the names of some of the people who help us in our everyday lives. For example:

1. People who look after our health: doctors, nurses, dentists.
2. People who look after our safety: firemen, policemen, ambulance men.
3. People who help us at home: milkmen, dustmen, postmen.
4. People who give us guidance and help: teachers, church leaders.
5. Friends and family who care for us and help us.

Finish with a prayer thanking God for all of these people, leaving pauses for the group to name silently people known to them personally.

99. Family tree

'Reverence for the Lord gives confidence and security to a man and his family.' Proverbs 14:26

Give each member of your group a simple outline of a person – a gingerbread man shape is ideal. Thread a piece of wool through a hole in the top of each figure. On one side of the figure invite people to write the names of all the people in their family. On the other side they could write a simple prayer, including any special needs and asking God to bless their family. Arrange a few branches in a vase and invite people to come up and hang their figure on the family tree. When everyone has done this a leader might like to say a final prayer, offering all these family prayers to God.

100. Prayer tree

'You soften the soil with showers and cause the young plants to grow.' Psalm 65:10

As for the family tree, you will need a few branches arranged in a vase. However, this time give each group member a leaf shape. Ask folk to use their prayer to write or draw something in God's creation for which they would like to say thank you. Put a spot of glue on one end of each leaf and stick the prayers to the branches of the tree.

101. Prayer boats

'Do not be afraid - I am with you!' Isaiah 43:5

Remind your group of the story of the storm on the lake (Matthew 8:23-27, Mark 2:1-12, Luke 5:17-26). When the disciples were afraid they turned to Jesus for help. When we are worried or afraid we can also turn to Jesus. Cut out a number of small boat shapes and invite your group to write on them a short prayer about anything that concerns or worries them. Have ready a simple outline of a lake and attach the boats to this picture with Blu-tack.

From time to time remember to ask the youngsters how Jesus has answered their prayer. Move the boats to the other side of the lake if the problem has been solved. This will give you the opportunity of talking about how some prayers are answered quickly, others slowly and some are prayers which God wants us to help answer by doing something ourselves.

(Geraldine Witcher)